Poison Antidotes

For all of vitriol or aquafortis give large doses of magnesia and water or equal parts of soft soap and water... ...magnesia or chalk... ...emetic of must... ...and female p... ...laudanum give en... ...tant motion if possib... ...nic doses of mag... ...and hydrate oxide... ...into the stomach down to emetic mercury of vinegar and salt. For corrosive sublimate give whites of eggs mixed with water until free vomiting takes place.

This Belongs To:

My Belief Statements

My Ritual or Spell

Date:

Name:

Purpose/Description:

Ingredients/Equipment

Feelings/Effects/Notes

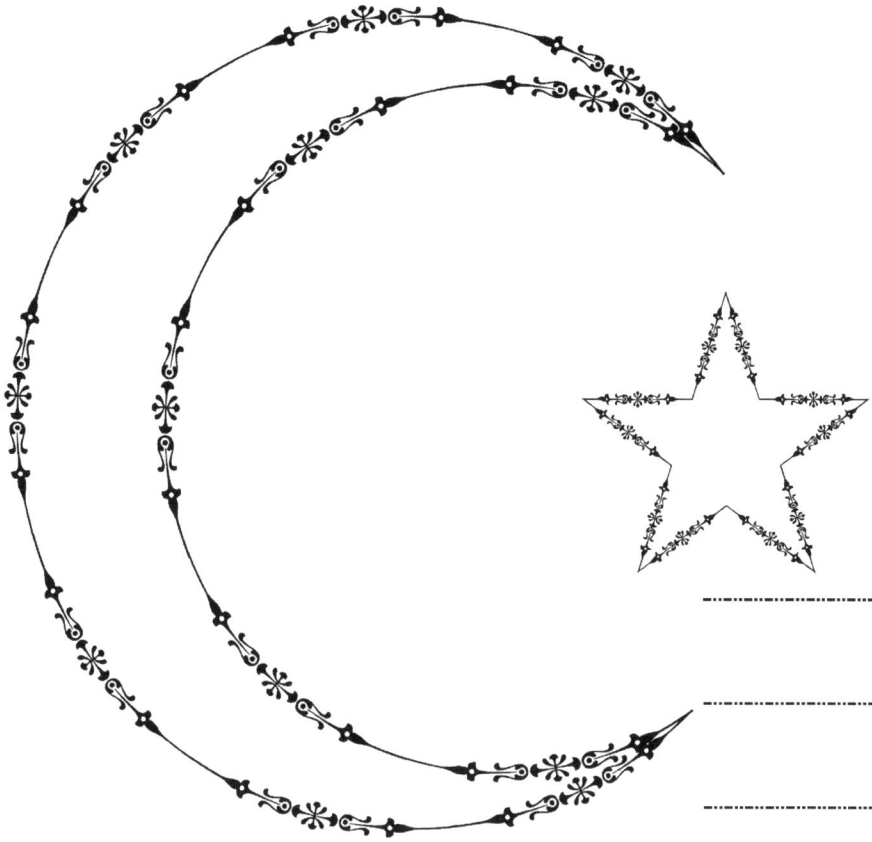

Dates

....

....

....

....

....

....

Manifestations, Results, Other Notations

My Ritual or Spell

Date:

Name:

Purpose/Description:

Ingredients/Equipment

· · · · · · · ·
·
· · · · · · · ·
·
· · · · · · · ·
·
· · · · · · · ·
·
· · · · · · · ·
·

Feelings/Effects/Notes

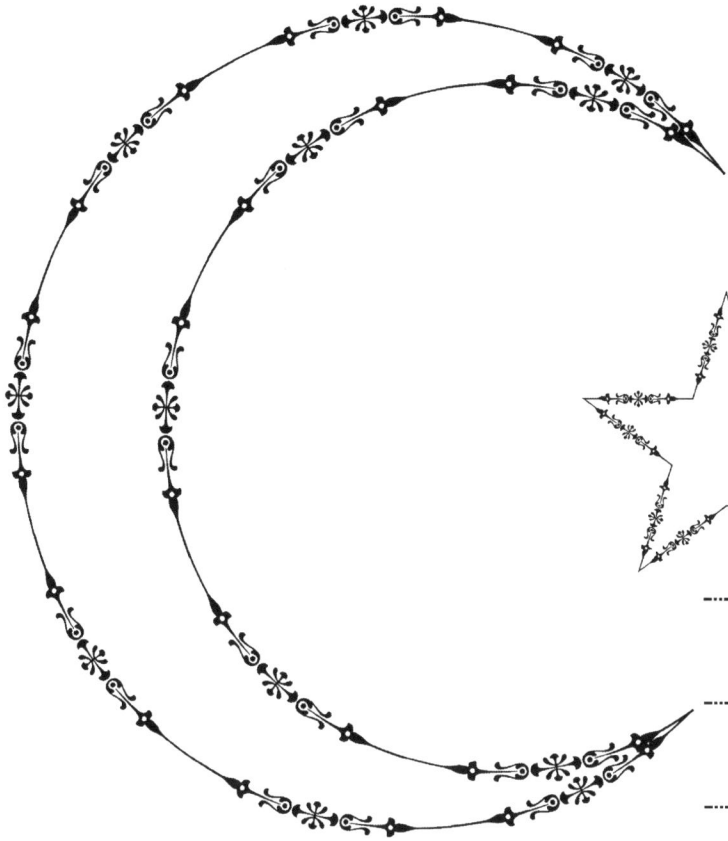

Dates

....

....

....

....

....

....

Manifestations, Results, Other Notations

My Ritual or Spell

Date:

Name:

Purpose/Description:

Ingredients/Equipment

Feelings/Effects/Notes

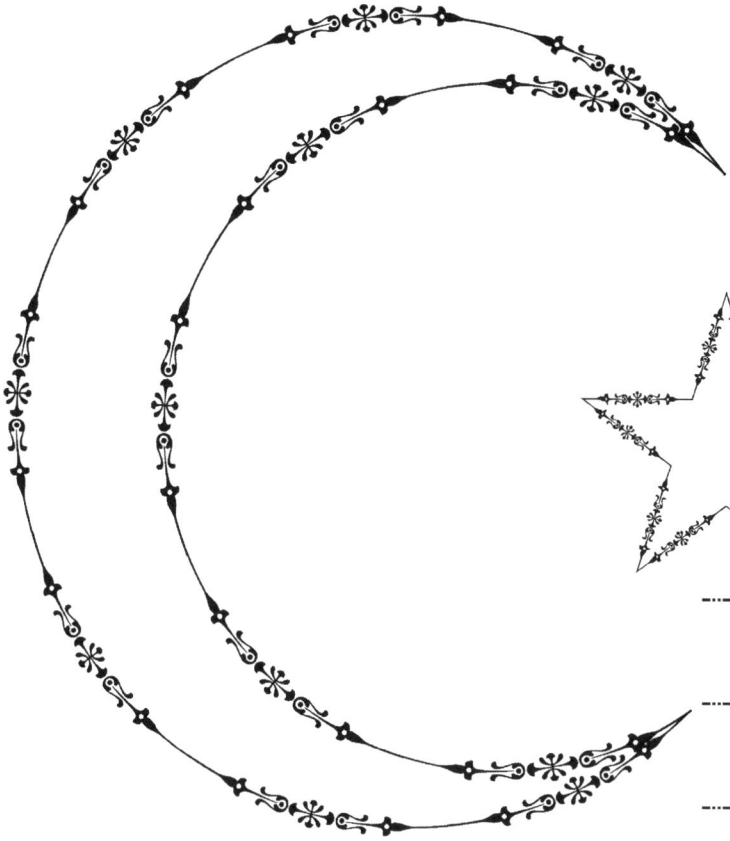

Dates

....

....

....

....

....

....

Manifestations, Results, Other Notations

My Ritual or Spell

Date:

Name:

Purpose/Description:

Ingredients/Equipment

Feelings/Effects/Notes

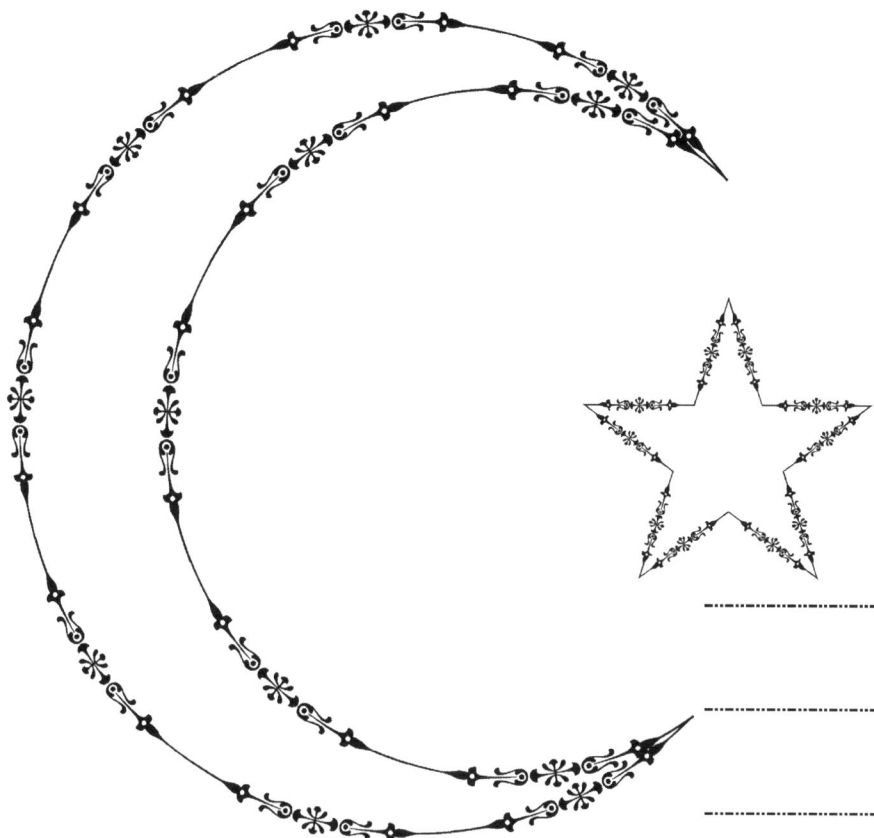

Dates

....

....

....

....

....

....

Manifestations, Results, Other Notations

....

....

....

....

....

....

....

My Ritual or Spell

Date:

Name:

Purpose/Description:

Ingredients/Equipment

Feelings/Effects/Notes

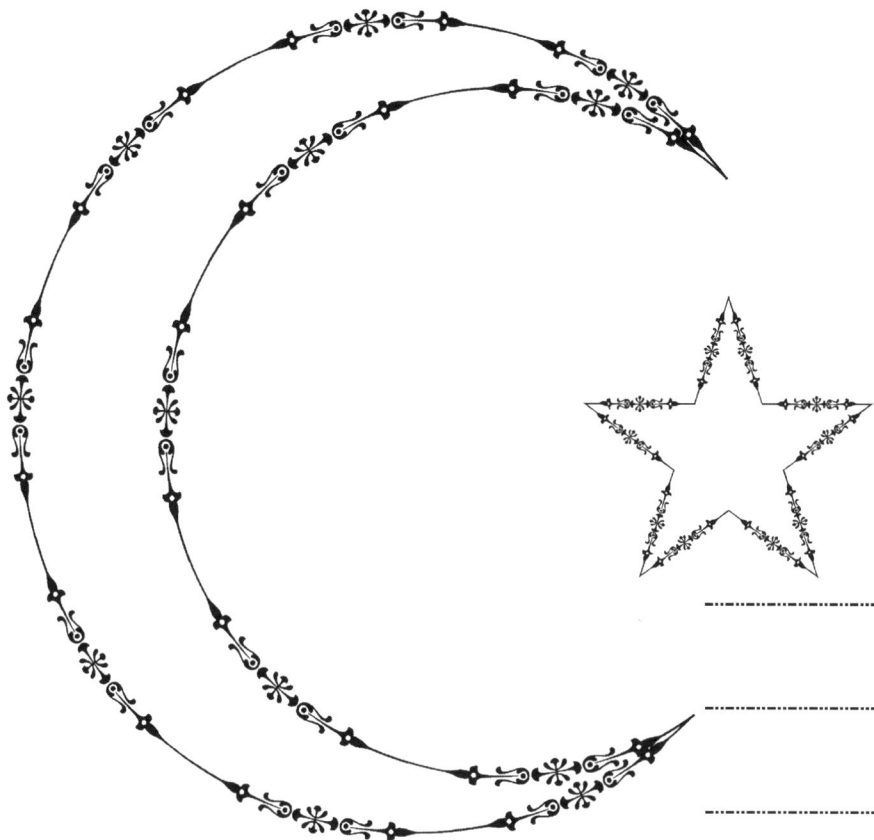

Dates

Manifestations, Results, Other Notations

My Ritual or Spell

Date:

Name:

Purpose/Description:

Ingredients/Equipment

-
-
-
-
-
-
-

Feelings/Effects/Notes

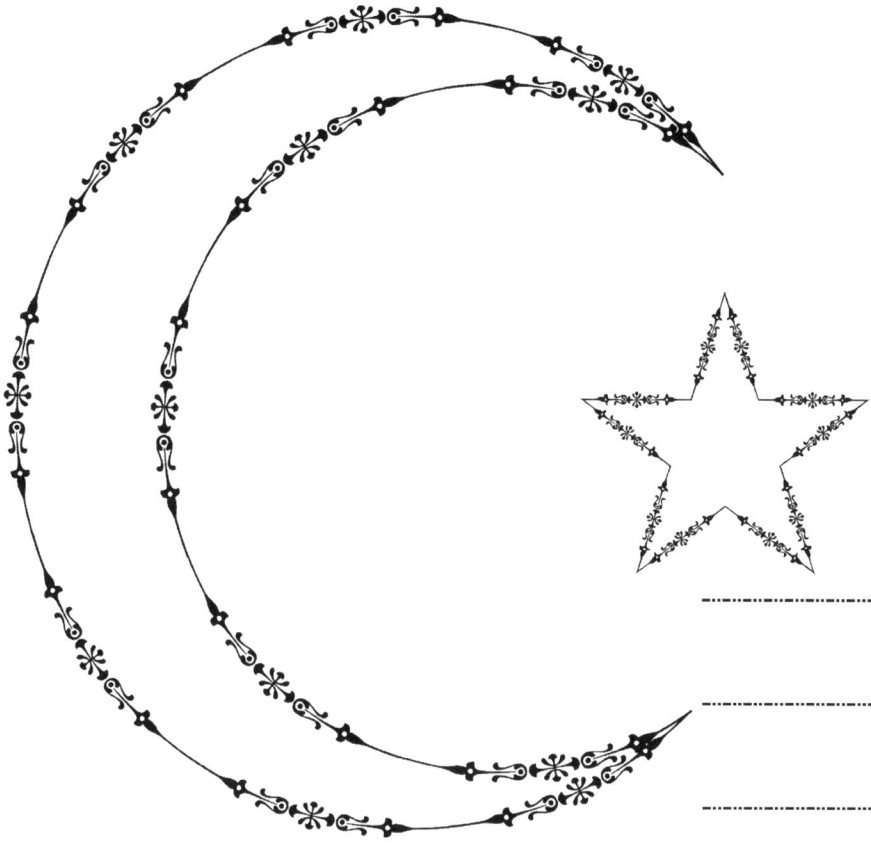

Dates

....

....

....

....

....

....

Manifestations, Results, Other Notations

My Ritual or Spell

Date:

Name:

Purpose/Description:

Ingredients/Equipment

Feelings/Effects/Notes

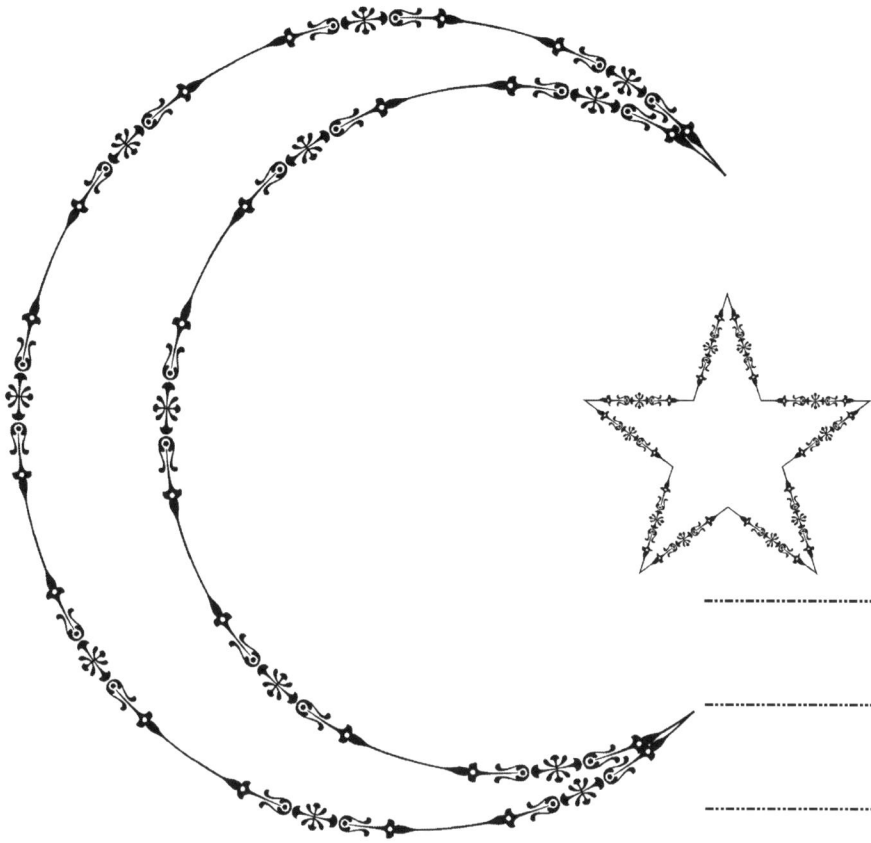

Dates
....
....
....
....
....
....

Manifestations, Results, Other Notations

My Ritual or Spell

Date:

Name:

Purpose/Description:

Ingredients/Equipment

Feelings/Effects/Notes

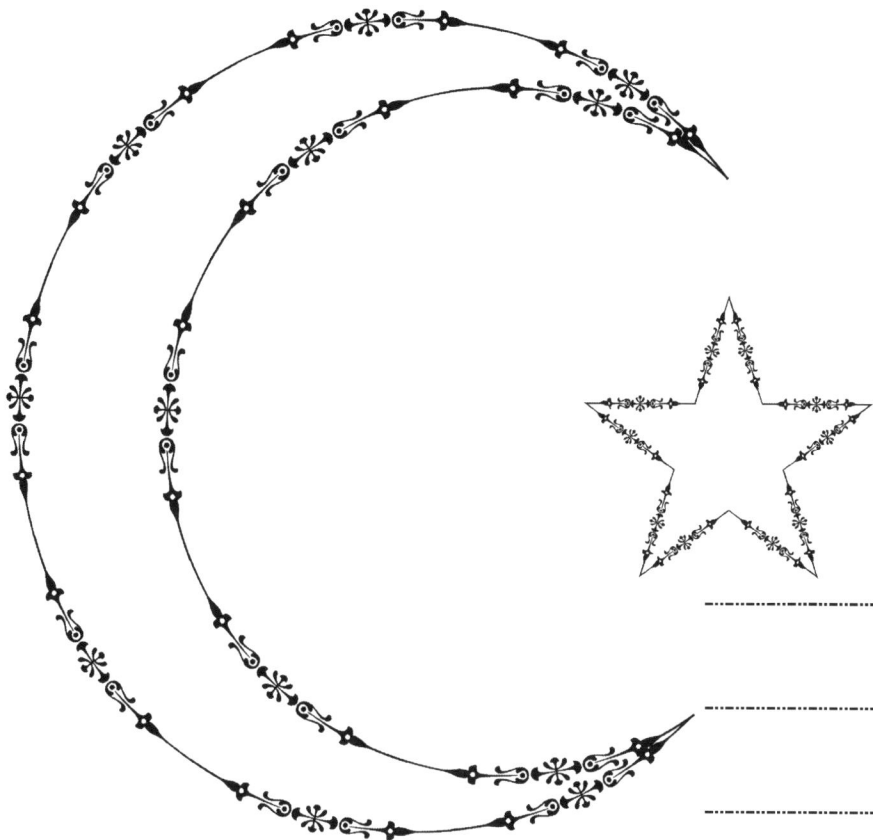

Dates

_____

_____

_____

_____

_____

_____

Manifestations, Results, Other Notations

My Ritual or Spell

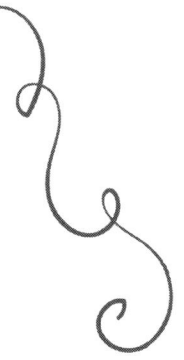

Date:

Name:

Purpose/Description:

Ingredients/Equipment

Feelings/Effects/Notes

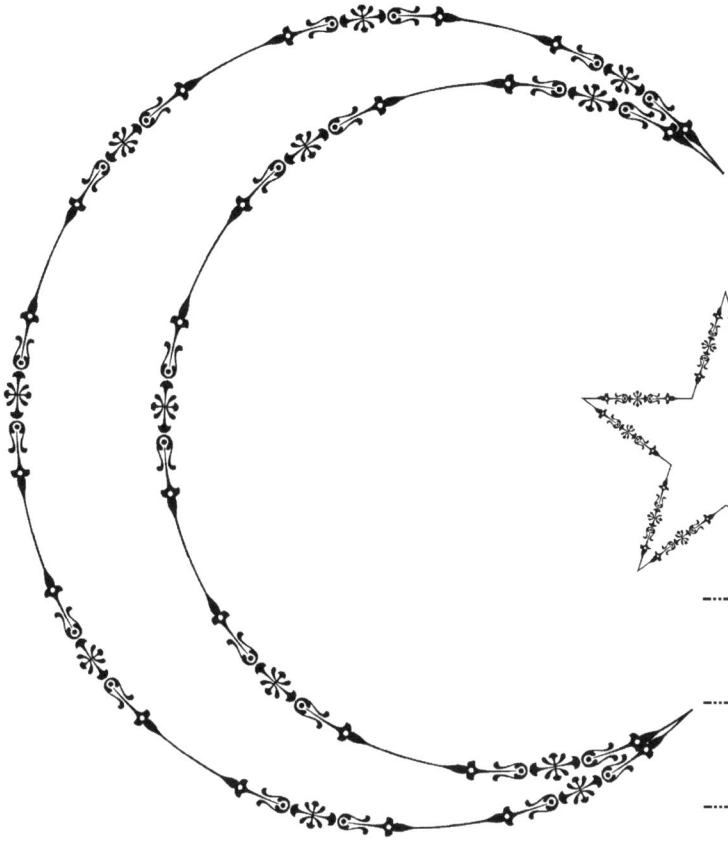

Dates

....

....

....

....

....

....

Manifestations, Results, Other Notations

My Ritual or Spell

Date:

Name:

Purpose/Description:

Ingredients/Equipment

-
-
-
-
-
-
-
-

Feelings/Effects/Notes

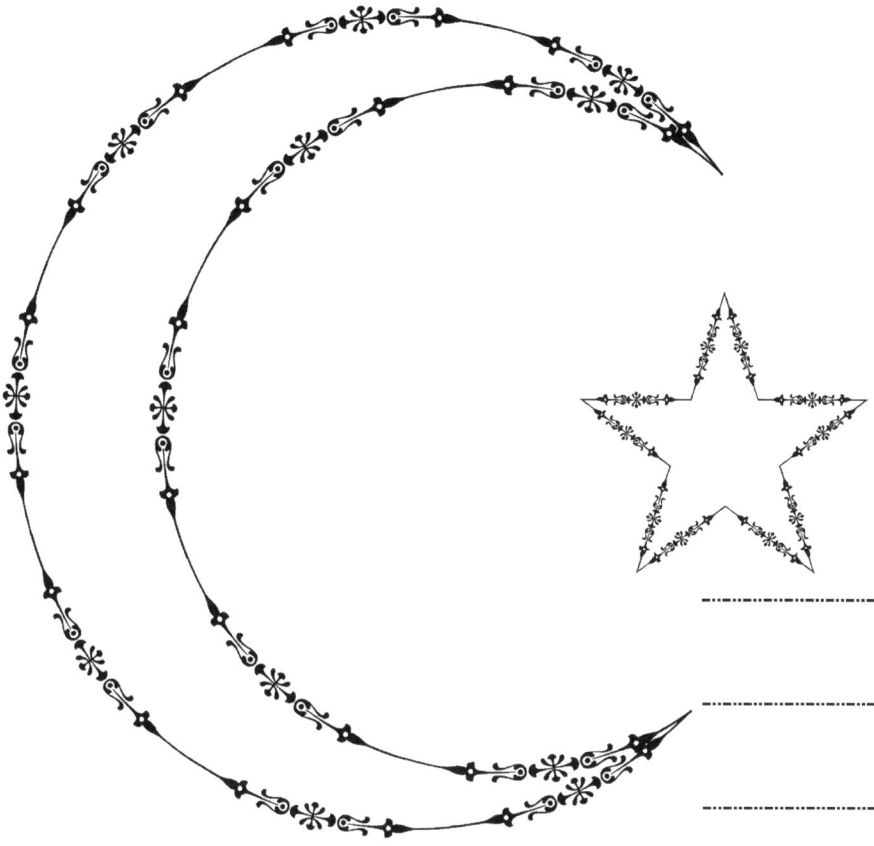

Dates

....

....

....

....

....

....

Manifestations, Results, Other Notations

My Ritual or Spell

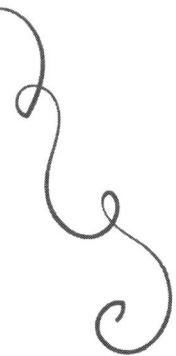

Date:

Name:

Purpose/Description:

Ingredients/Equipment

Feelings/Effects/Notes

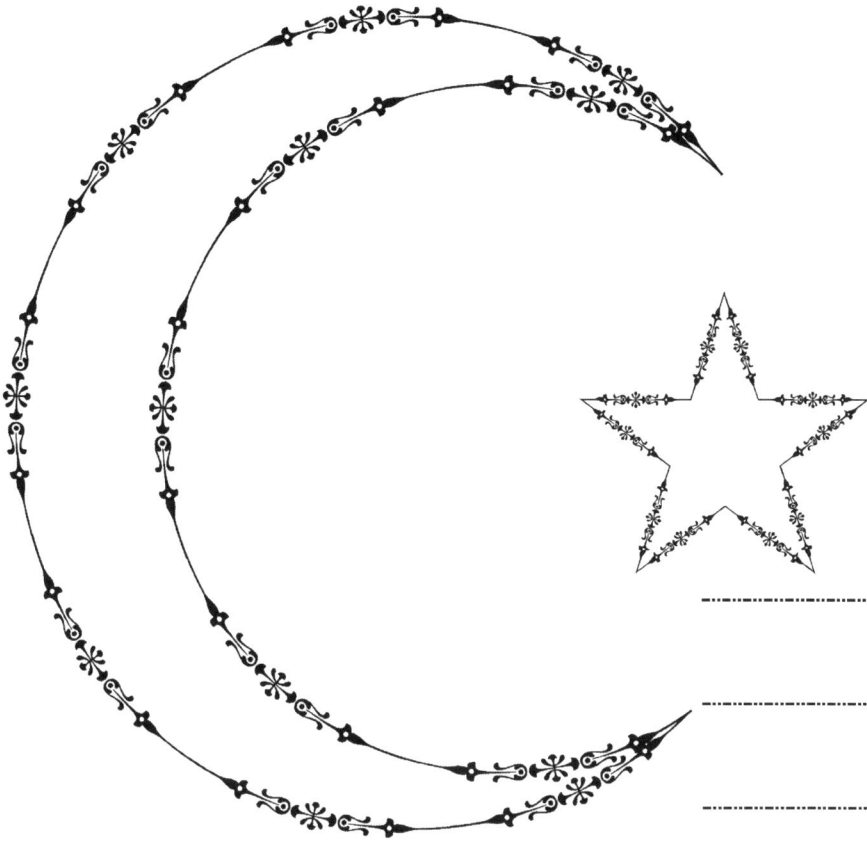

Dates

....

....

....

....

....

....

Manifestations, Results, Other Notations

....

....

....

....

....

....

....

My Ritual or Spell

Date:

Name:

Purpose/Description:

Ingredients/Equipment

-
-
-
-
-
-
-

Feelings/Effects/Notes

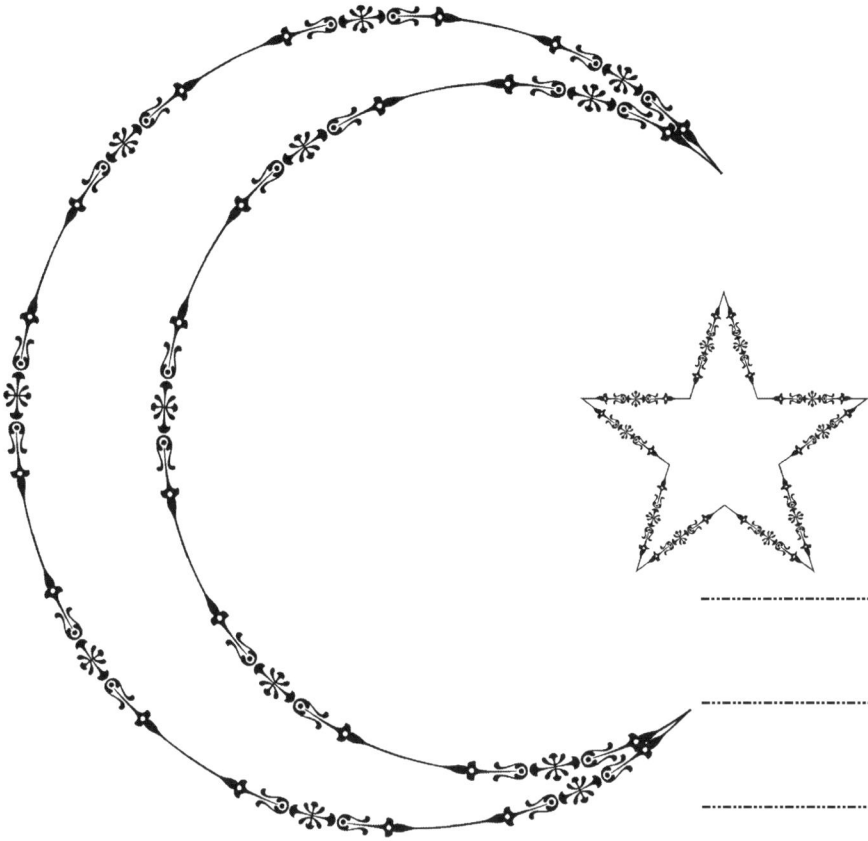

Dates

Manifestations, Results, Other Notations

My Ritual or Spell

Date:

Name:

Purpose/Description:

Ingredients/Equipment

. . . .
        .
. . . .
        .
. . . .
        .
. . . .
        .
. . . .
        .

Feelings/Effects/Notes

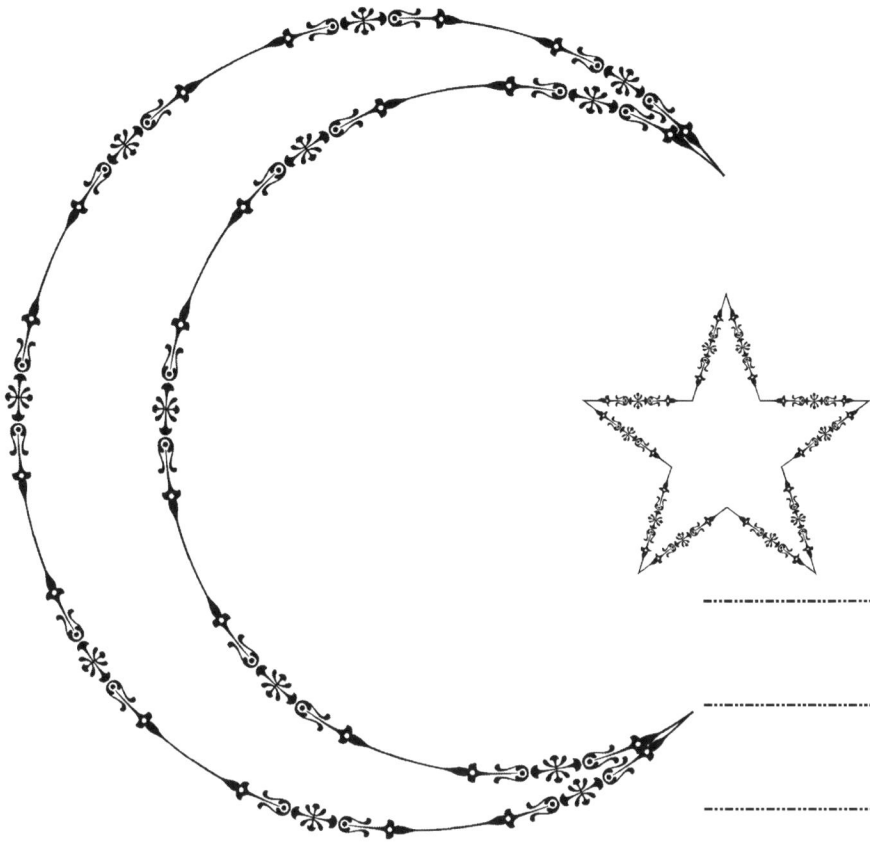

Dates

....

....

....

....

....

....

Manifestations, Results, Other Notations

My Ritual or Spell

Date:

Name:

Purpose/Description:

Ingredients/Equipment

Feelings/Effects/Notes

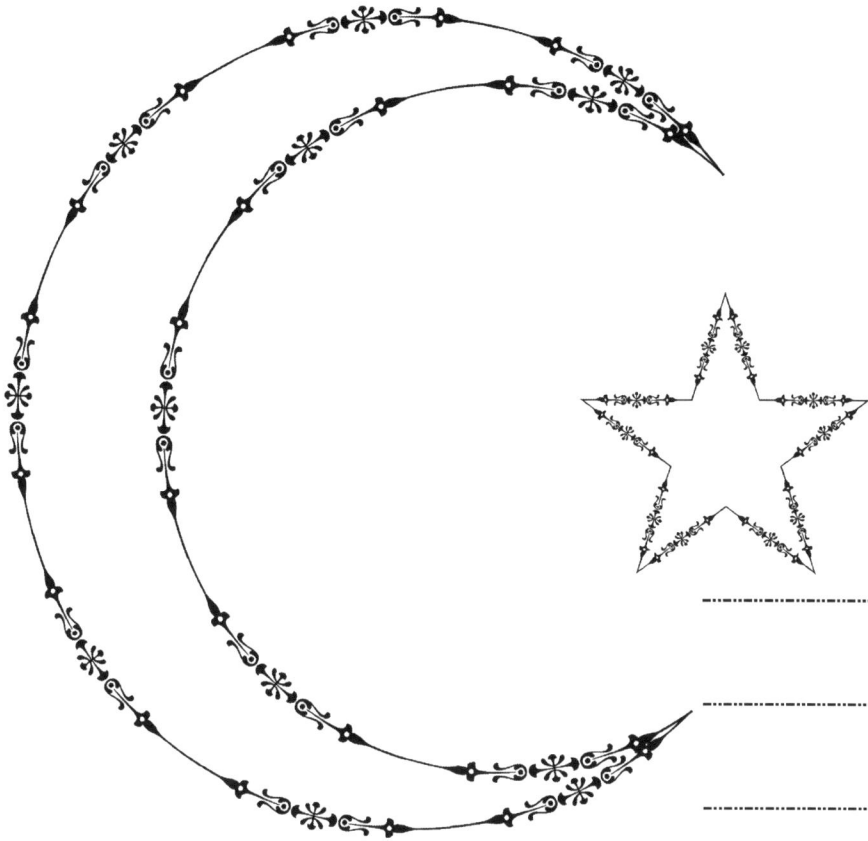

Dates

....

....

....

....

....

....

Manifestations, Results, Other Notations

My Ritual or Spell

Date:

Name:

Purpose/Description:

Ingredients/Equipment

· · · · · · · · ·
·
· · · · · · · · ·
·
· · · · · · · · ·
·
· · · · · · · · ·
·
· · · · · · · · ·

Feelings/Effects/Notes

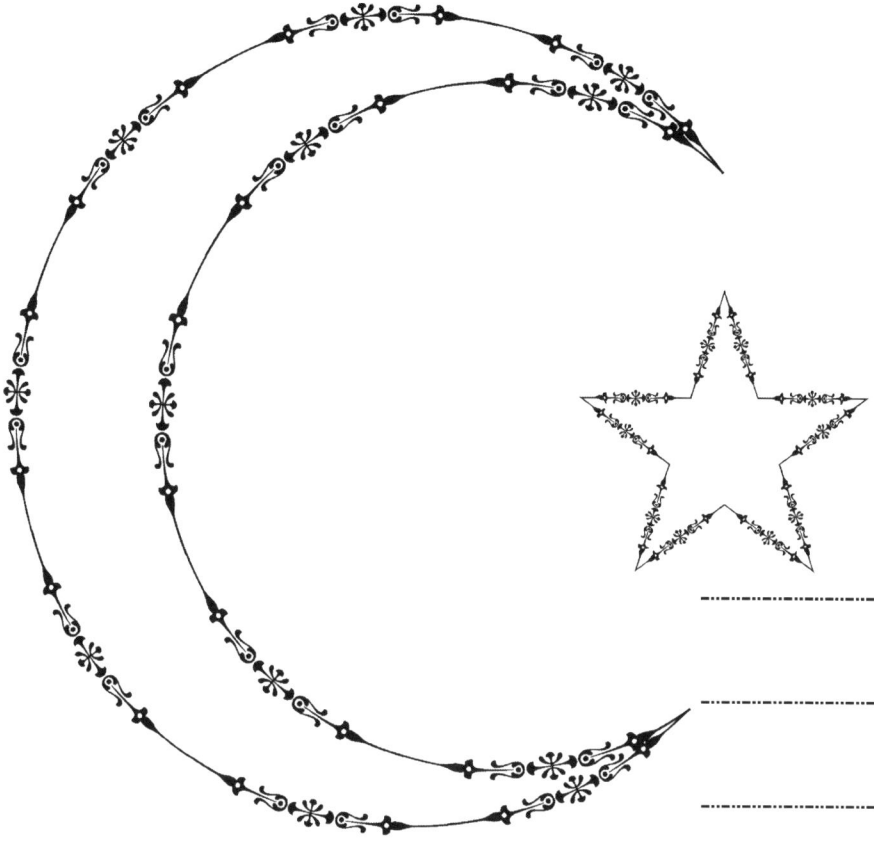

Dates

....

....

....

....

....

....

Manifestations, Results, Other Notations

....

....

....

....

....

....

....

My Ritual or Spell

Date:

Name:

Purpose/Description:

Ingredients/Equipment

- · · · · · · · · ·
- ·
- · · · · · · · · ·
- ·
- · · · · · · · · ·
- ·
- · · · · · · · · ·
- ·
- · · · · · · · · ·

Feelings/Effects/Notes

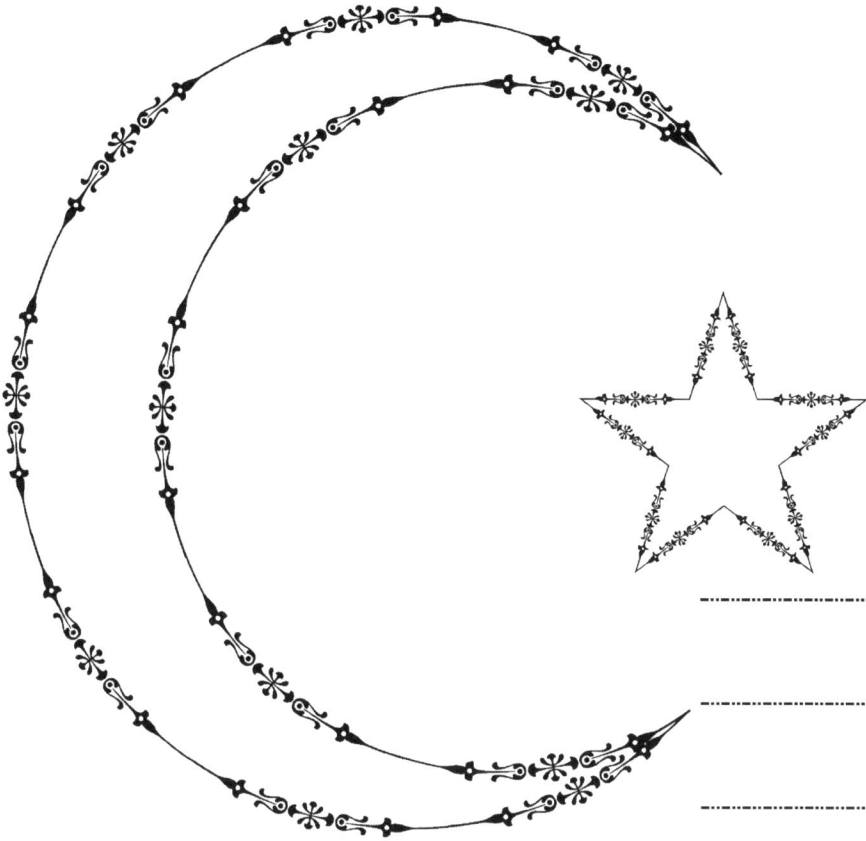

Dates
....
....
....
....
....
....

Manifestations, Results, Other Notations

My Ritual or Spell

Date:

Name:

Purpose/Description:

Ingredients/Equipment

Feelings/Effects/Notes

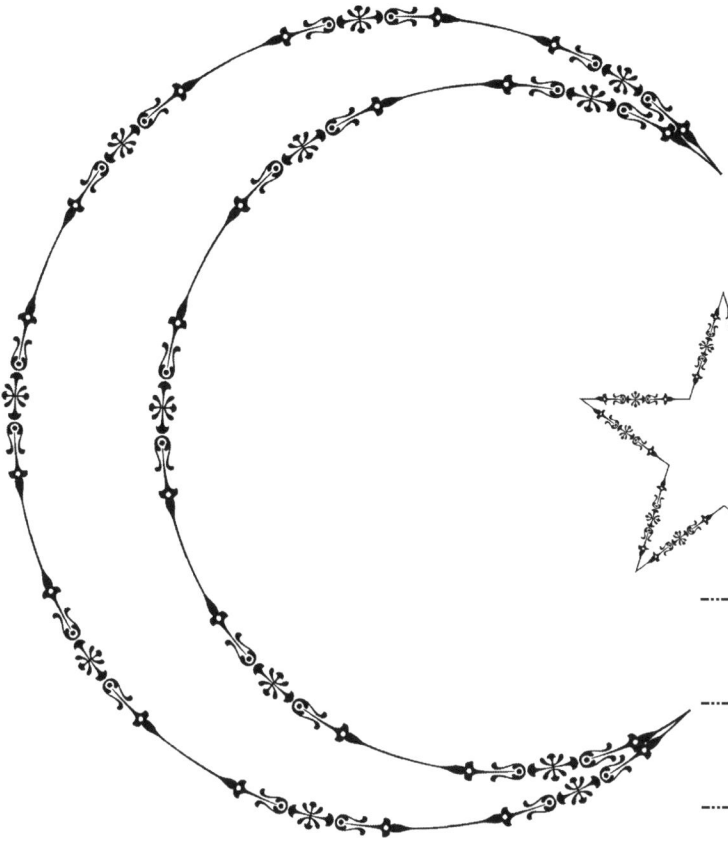

Dates

Manifestations, Results, Other Notations

My Ritual or Spell

Date:

Name:

Purpose/Description:

Ingredients/Equipment

· · · · · · · · ·

·

· · · · · · · · ·

·

· · · · · · · · ·

·

· · · · · · · · ·

·

· · · · · · · · ·

Feelings/Effects/Notes

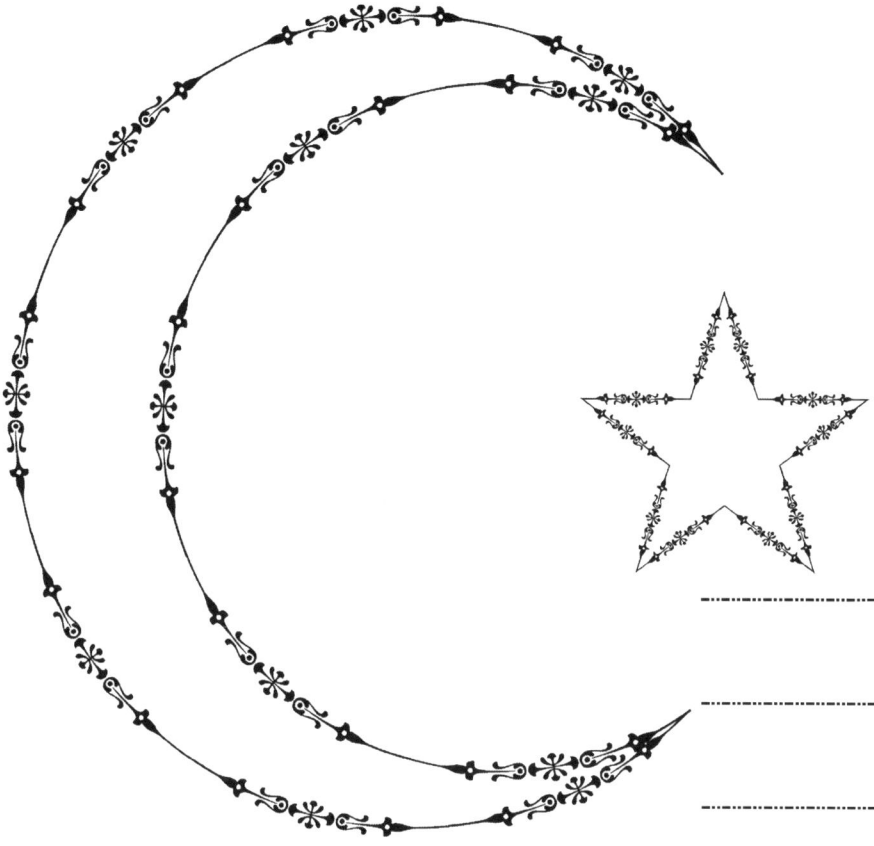

Dates

....

....

....

....

....

....

Manifestations, Results, Other Notations

My Ritual or Spell

Date:

Name:

Purpose/Description:

Ingredients/Equipment

- · · · · · · · ·
- ·
- · · · · · · · ·
- ·
- · · · · · · · ·
- ·
- · · · · · · · ·
- ·
- · · · · · · · ·
- ·

Feelings/Effects/Notes

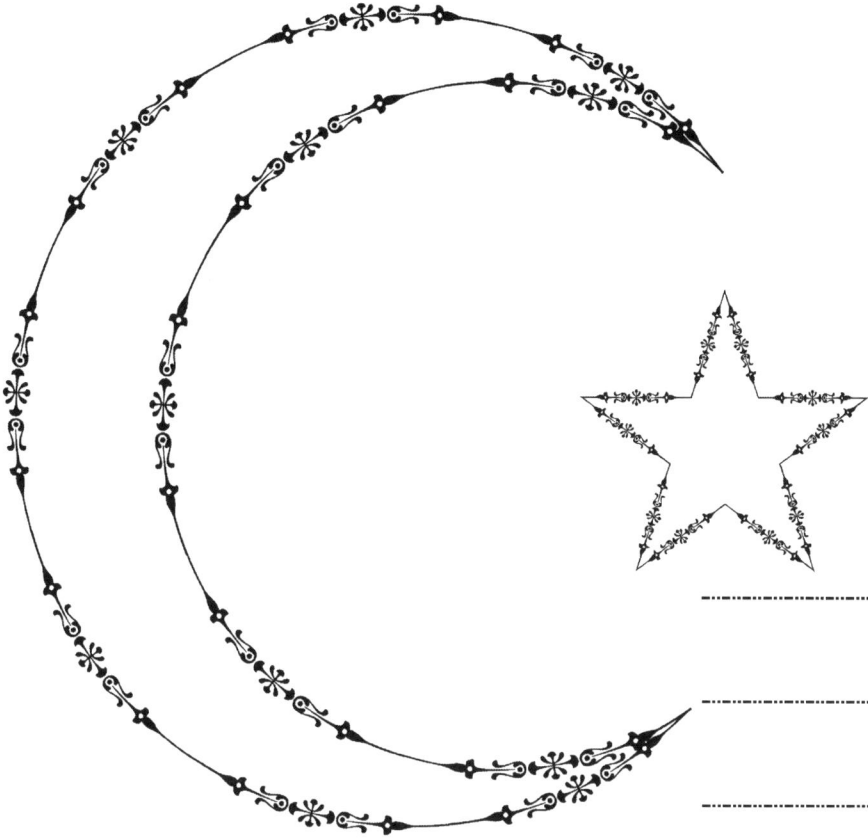

Dates

....

....

....

....

....

....

Manifestations, Results, Other Notations

My Ritual or Spell

Date:

Name:

Purpose/Description:

Ingredients/Equipment

- - - - - - - - - -
                -
- - - - - - - - - -
                -
- - - - - - - - - -
                -
- - - - - - - - - -
                -
- - - - - - - - - -
                -

Feelings/Effects/Notes

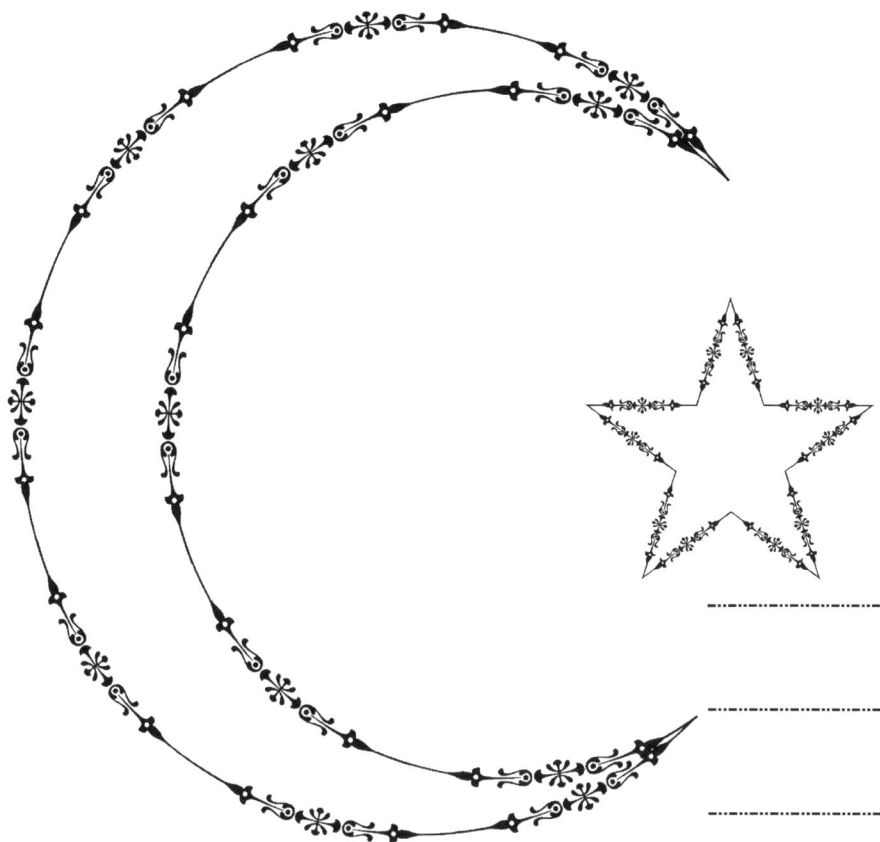

Dates

....

....

....

....

....

....

Manifestations, Results, Other Notations

My Ritual or Spell

Date:

Name:

Purpose/Description:

Ingredients/Equipment

Feelings/Effects/Notes

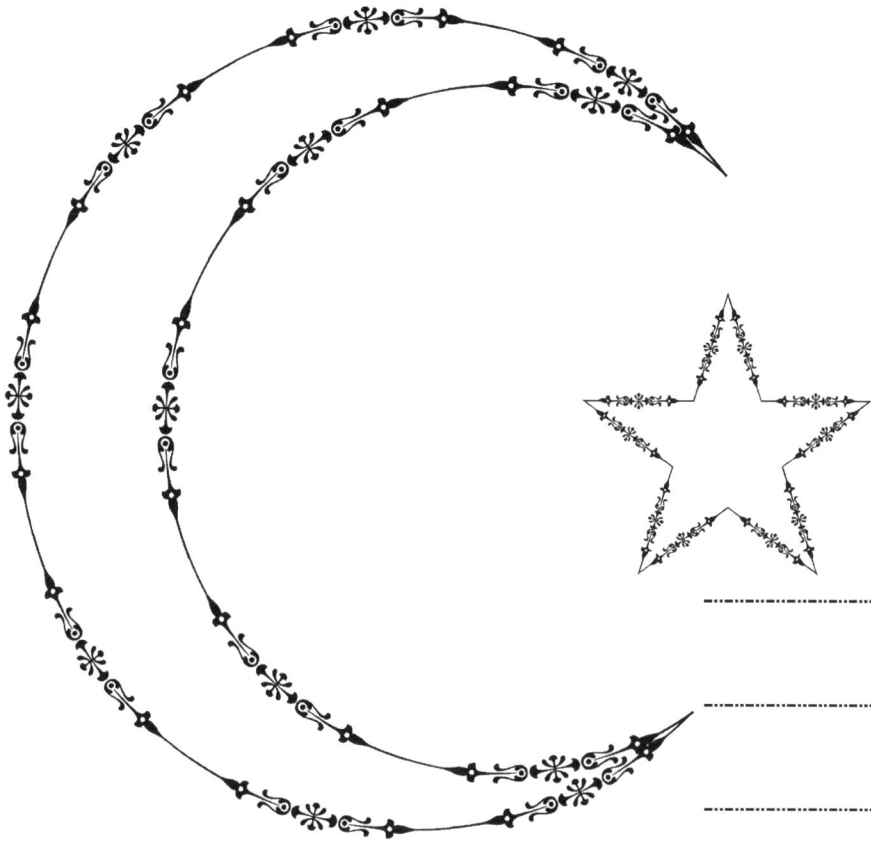

Dates

....

....

....

....

....

....

Manifestations, Results, Other Notations

Best Weekday for Spells and Rituals

Mon	Ruling Planet is the Moon. Good for invoking power, healing, creative ideas, and impressions.
Tue	Ruling Planet is Mars. Good for protection, confidence, a strong body and mind, and sexual encounters.
Wed	Ruling Planet is Mercury. Good for learning, research, job and career, and travel plans.
Thurs	Ruling Planet is Jupiter. Good for deeper spirituality and personal development, and money or legal concerns.
Fri	Ruling Planet is Venus. Good for beautifying yourself and surroundings, reconciling relationships and romantic attractions.
Sat	Ruling Planet is Saturn. Good for releasing negativity in self or relationships, home issues, personal goals and weight loss.
Sun	Ruling Planet is the Sun. Good for decision-making and problem solving, friendships, divine interventions, and healing of body, mind, and soul.

Crystals &
Use/Properties

Crystals I
Use/Properties

Crystals &
Use/Properties

Crystals &
Use/Properties

Crystals &
Use/Properties

Crystals &
Use/Properties

Spells for Certain Times of the Day

Dawning

_____

_____

_____

_____

_____

_____

_____

_____

_____

_____

_____

_____

_____

Dawning

Noontime

_____

_____

_____

_____

_____

_____

_____

_____

_____

_____

_____

Noontime

Setting Sun

_____

_____

_____

_____

_____

_____

_____

_____

_____

_____

_____

_____

Setting Sun

_____

_____

_____

_____

_____

_____

_____

_____

_____

_____

_____

_____

Setting Sun

_____

_____

_____

_____

_____

_____

_____

_____

_____

_____

_____

_____

Dark of
Night

Dark of
Night

_____

_____

_____

_____

_____

_____

_____

_____

_____

_____

_____

Dark of

Night

_____

_____

_____

_____

_____

_____

_____

_____

_____

_____

_____

_____

Chants, Affirmations

Chants, Affirmations

Chants, Affirmations

Chants, Affirmations

Chants, Affirmations

Chants, Affirmations

Chants, Affirmations

Chants, Affirmations

Chants, Affirmations

Chants, Affirmations

Chants, Affirmations

Chants, Affirmations

Chants, Affirmations

Chants, Affirmations

Chants, Affirmations

Chants, Affirmations

Chants, Affirmations

Chants, Affirmations

Chants, Affirmations

Chants, Affirmations

Chants, Affirmations

Chants, Affirmations

Chants, Affirmations

Lunar Phases

Lunar Phases

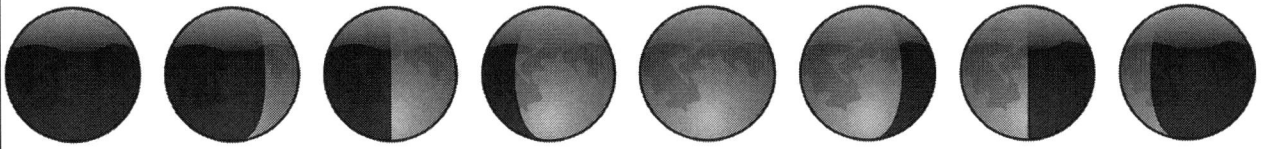

1	2	3	4	5	6
7	8	9	10	11	12
13	14	15	16	17	18
19	20	21	22	23	24
25	26	27	28	29	30

Lunar Phases

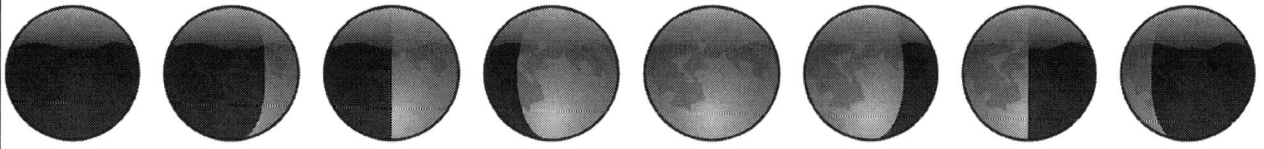

1	2	3	4	5	6
7	8	9	10	11	12
13	14	15	16	17	18
19	20	21	22	23	24
25	26	27	28	29	30

Lunar Phases

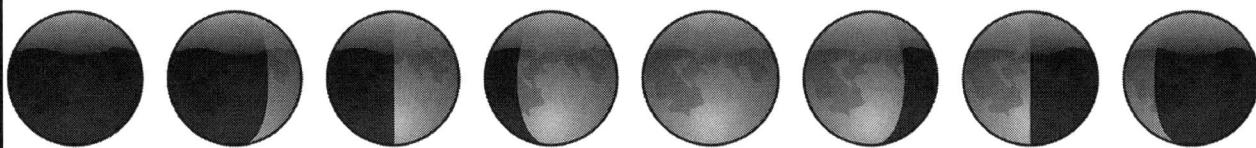

1	2	3	4	5	6
7	8	9	10	11	12
13	14	15	16	17	18
19	20	21	22	23	24
25	26	27	28	29	30

Lunar Phases

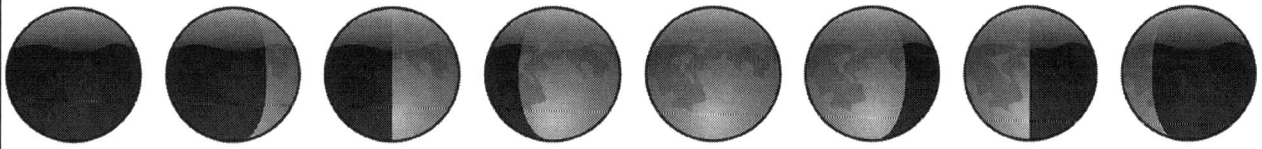

1	2	3	4	5	6
7	8	9	10	11	12
13	14	15	16	17	18
19	20	21	22	23	24
25	26	27	28	29	30

Lunar Phases

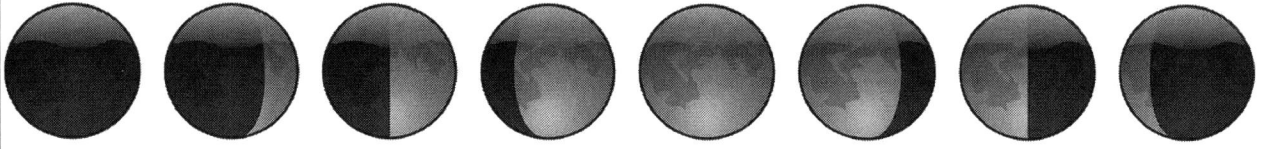

1	2	3	4	5	6
7	8	9	10	11	12
13	14	15	16	17	18
19	20	21	22	23	24
25	26	27	28	29	30

Lunar Phases

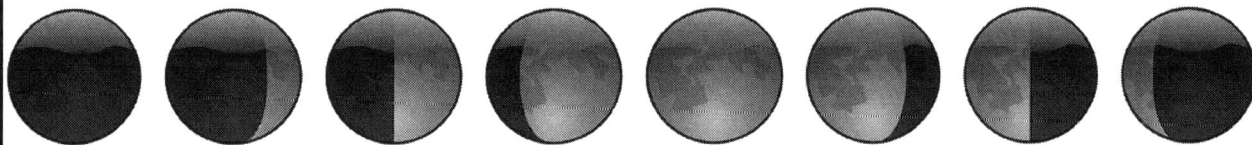

1	2	3	4	5	6
7	8	9	10	11	12
13	14	15	16	17	18
19	20	21	22	23	24
25	26	27	28	29	30

Lunar Phases

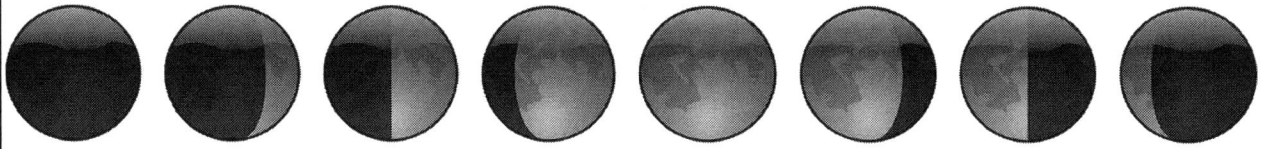

1	2	3	4	5	6
7	8	9	10	11	12
13	14	15	16	17	18
19	20	21	22	23	24
25	26	27	28	29	30

Lunar Phases

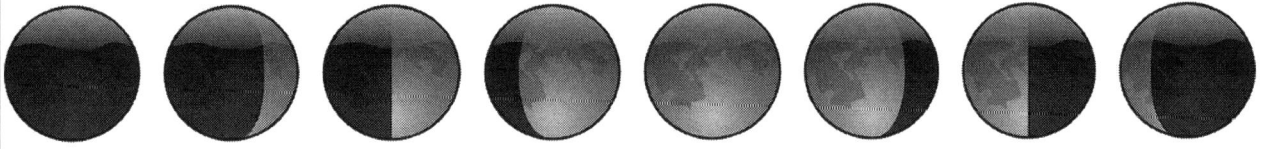

1	2	3	4	5	6
7	8	9	10	11	12
13	14	15	16	17	18
19	20	21	22	23	24
25	26	27	28	29	30

Lunar Phases

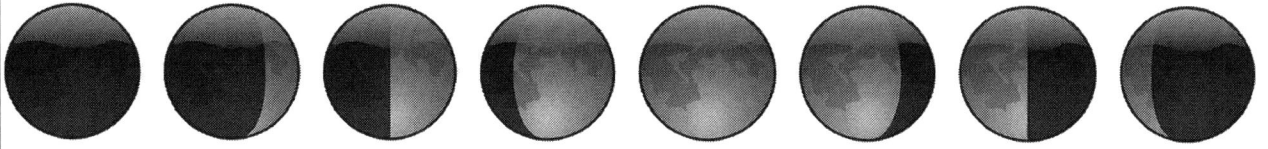

1	2	3	4	5	6
7	8	9	10	11	12
13	14	15	16	17	18
19	20	21	22	23	24
25	26	27	28	29	30

Lunar Phases

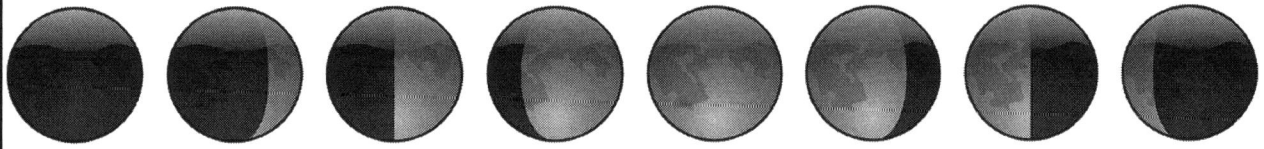

1	2	3	4	5	6
7	8	9	10	11	12
13	14	15	16	17	18
19	20	21	22	23	24
25	26	27	28	29	30

Lunar Phases

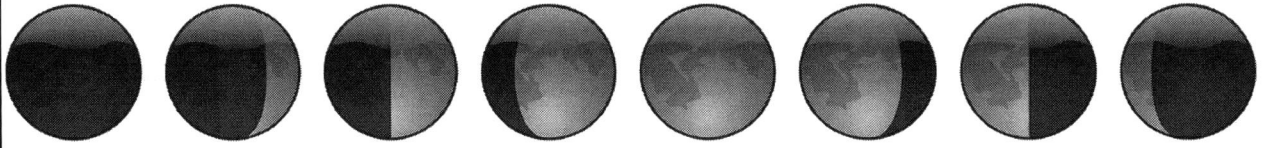

1	2	3	4	5	6
7	8	9	10	11	12
13	14	15	16	17	18
19	20	21	22	23	24
25	26	27	28	29	30

Lunar Phases

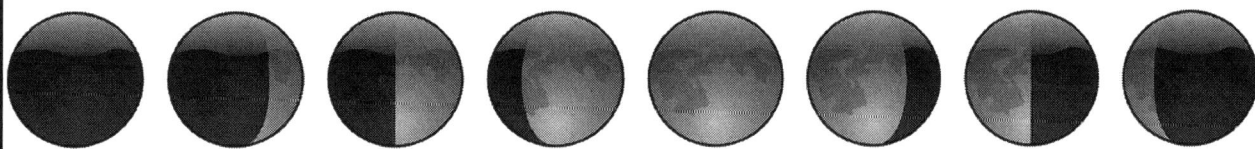

1	2	3	4	5	6
7	8	9	10	11	12
13	14	15	16	17	18
19	20	21	22	23	24
25	26	27	28	29	30

Lunar Phases

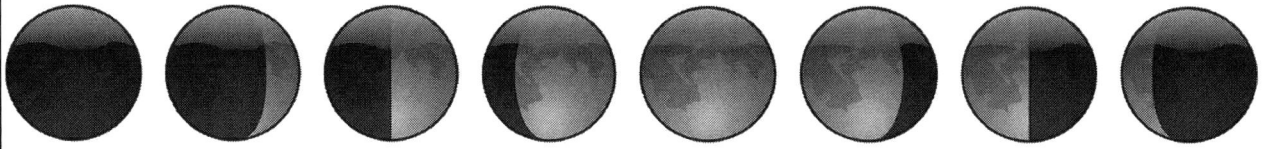

1	2	3	4	5	6
7	8	9	10	11	12
13	14	15	16	17	18
19	20	21	22	23	24
25	26	27	28	29	30

Lunar Phases

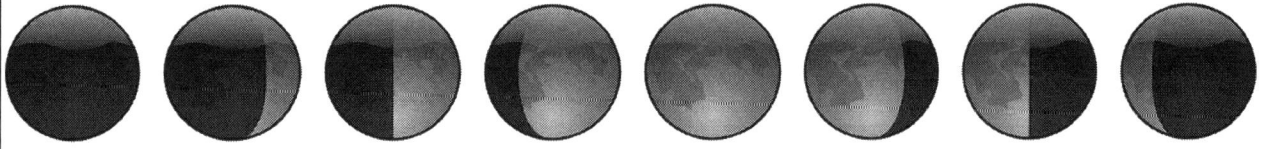

1	2	3	4	5	6
7	8	9	10	11	12
13	14	15	16	17	18
19	20	21	22	23	24
25	26	27	28	29	30

Lunar Phases

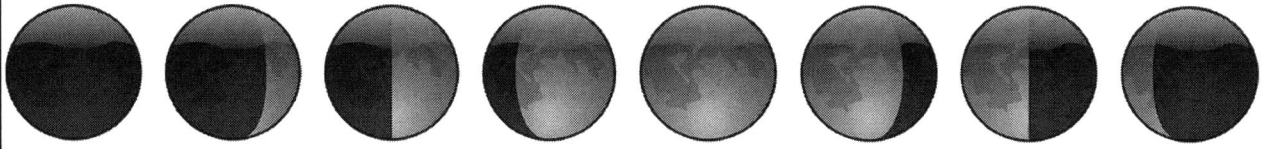

1	2	3	4	5	6
7	8	9	10	11	12
13	14	15	16	17	18
19	20	21	22	23	24
25	26	27	28	29	30

Lunar Phases

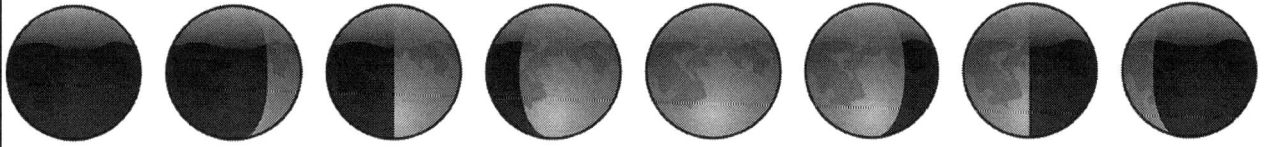

1	2	3	4	5	6
7	8	9	10	11	12
13	14	15	16	17	18
19	20	21	22	23	24
25	26	27	28	29	30

Lunar Phases

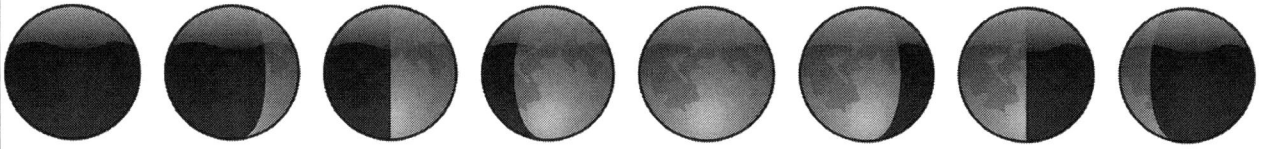

1	2	3	4	5	6
7	8	9	10	11	12
13	14	15	16	17	18
19	20	21	22	23	24
25	26	27	28	29	30

Lunar Phases

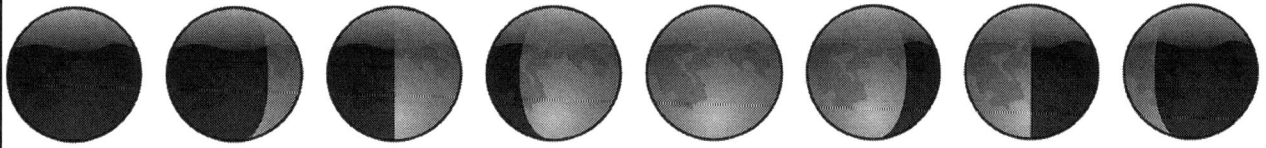

1	2	3	4	5	6
7	8	9	10	11	12
13	14	15	16	17	18
19	20	21	22	23	24
25	26	27	28	29	30

Lunar Phases

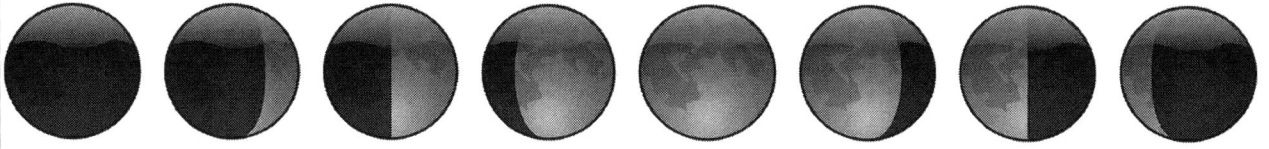

1	2	3	4	5	6
7	8	9	10	11	12
13	14	15	16	17	18
19	20	21	22	23	24
25	26	27	28	29	30

Lunar Phases

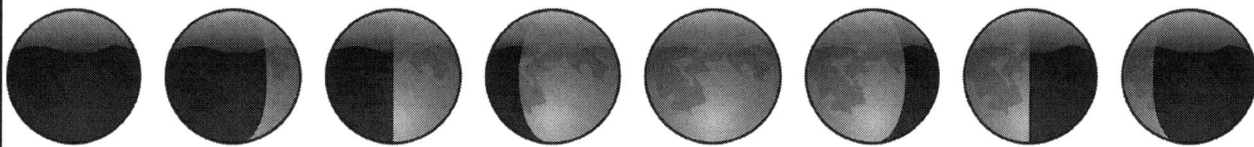

1	2	3	4	5	6
7	8	9	10	11	12
13	14	15	16	17	18
19	20	21	22	23	24
25	26	27	28	29	30

Lunar Phases

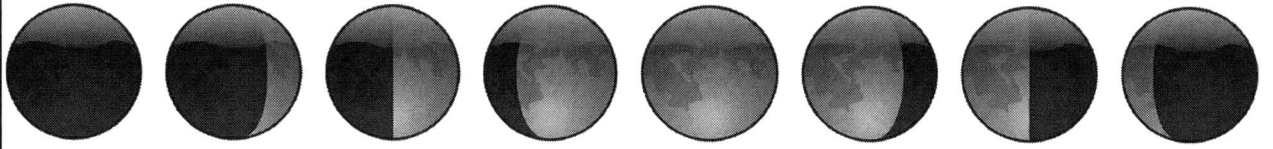

1	2	3	4	5	6
7	8	9	10	11	12
13	14	15	16	17	18
19	20	21	22	23	24
25	26	27	28	29	30

Lunar Phases

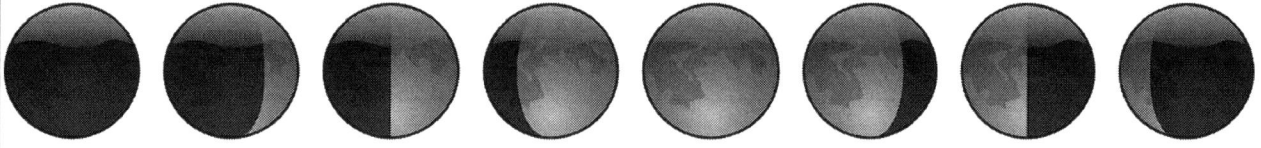

1	2	3	4	5	6
7	8	9	10	11	12
13	14	15	16	17	18
19	20	21	22	23	24
25	26	27	28	29	30

Lunar Phases

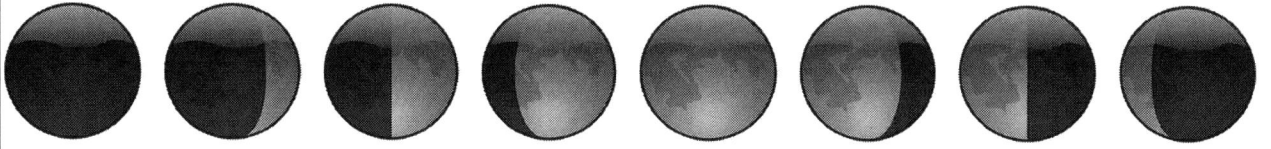

1	2	3	4	5	6
7	8	9	10	11	12
13	14	15	16	17	18
19	20	21	22	23	24
25	26	27	28	29	30

Lunar Phases

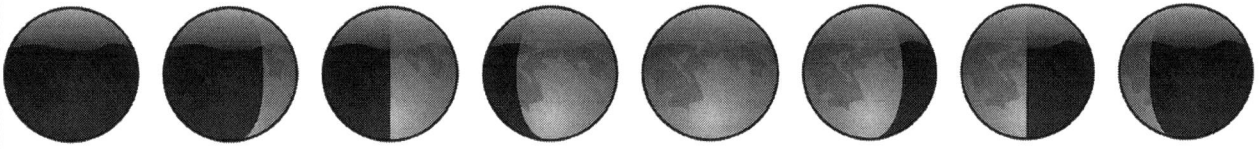

1	2	3	4	5	6
7	8	9	10	11	12
13	14	15	16	17	18
19	20	21	22	23	24
25	26	27	28	29	30

Special Poems

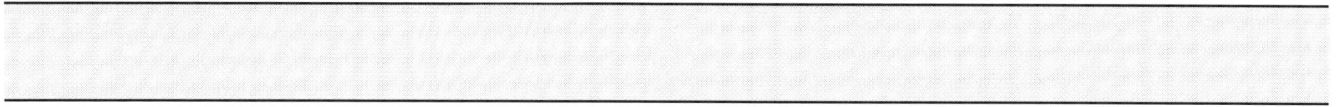

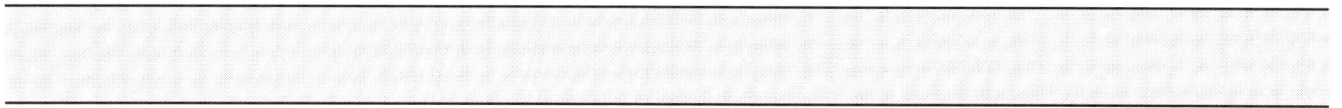

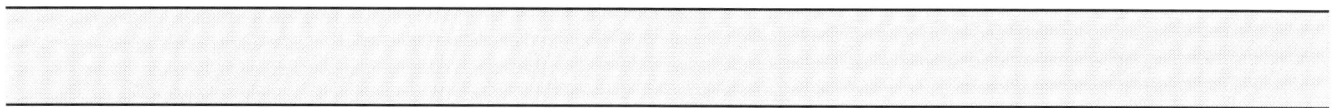

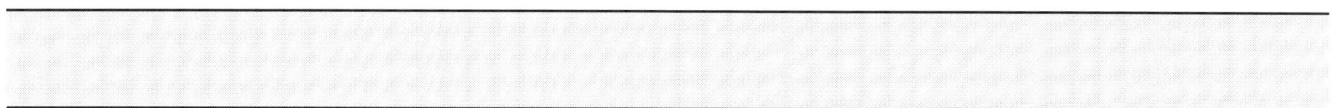

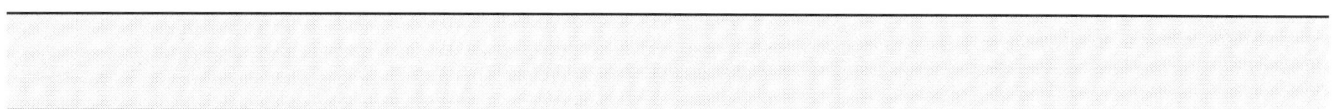

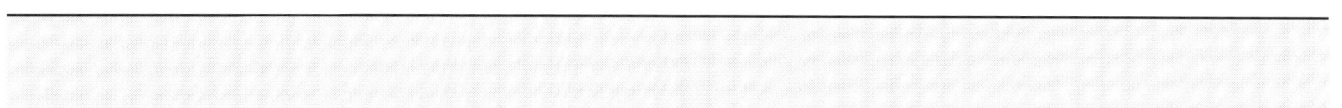

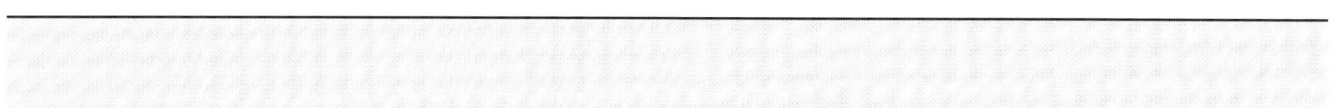

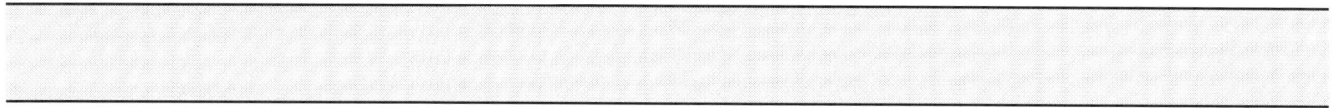

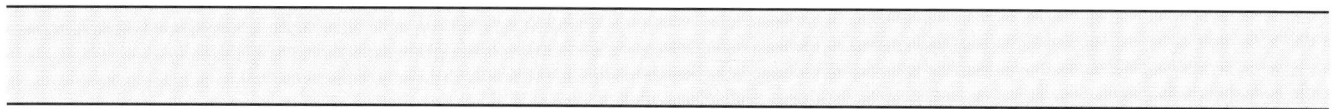

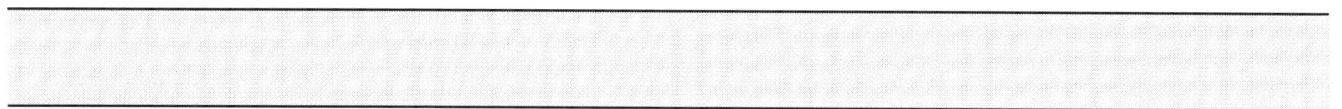

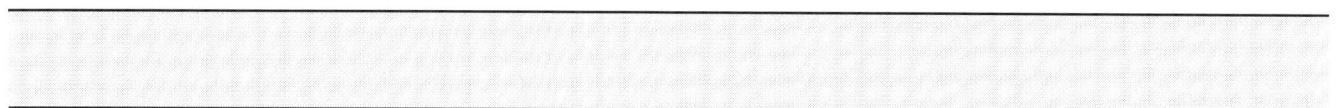

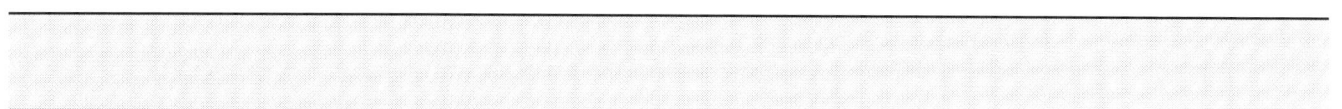

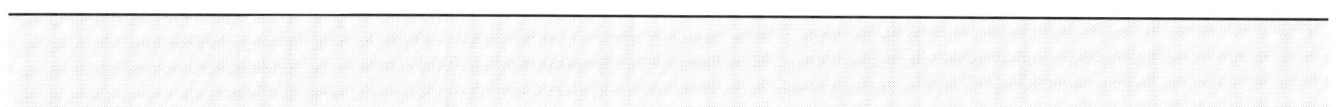

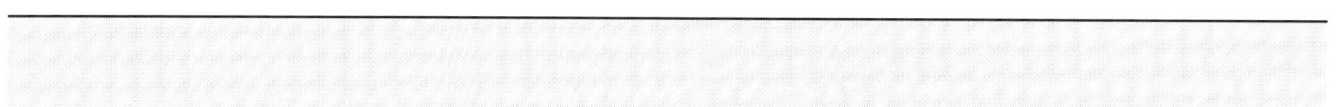

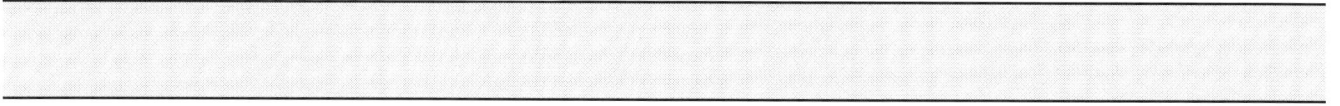

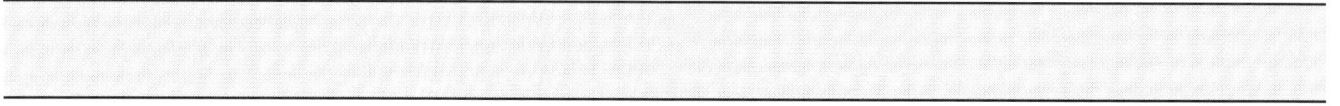

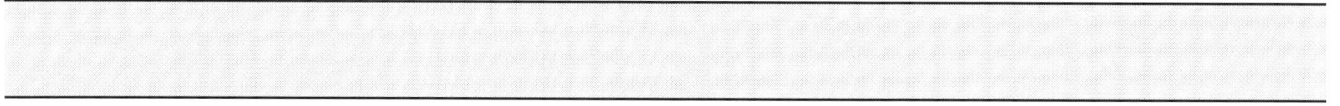

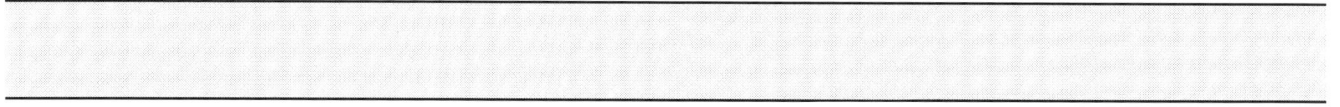

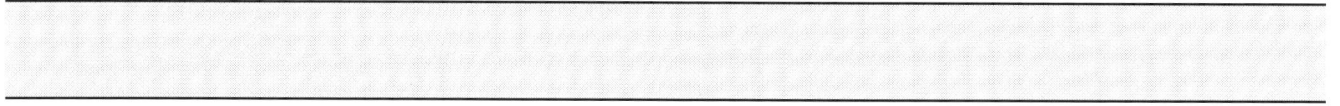

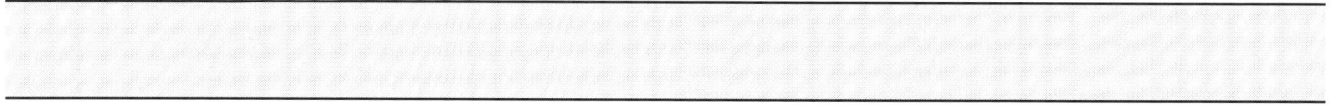

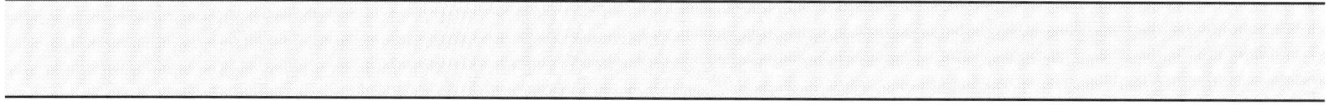

Stories

My Art

Made in the USA
Las Vegas, NV
13 December 2021